I SPY
ULTIMATE
CHALLENGER!

A BOOK OF
PICTURE
RIDDLES

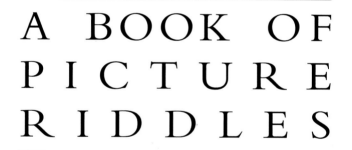

Photographs by Walter Wick

Riddles by Jean Marzollo

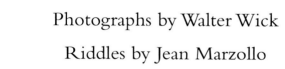

Cartwheel
·B·O·O·K·S·®

SCHOLASTIC INC.

New York   Toronto   London   Auckland   Sydney
Mexico City   New Delhi   Hong Kong   Buenos Aires

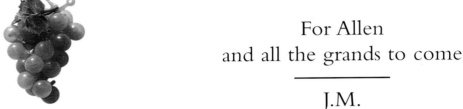

To Eva and
Margot Kempezynski

———

W.W.

For Allen
and all the grands to come

———

J.M.

Book design by Carol Devine Carson

Text copyright © 2003 by Jean Marzollo.
All rights reserved. Published by Scholastic Inc.
SCHOLASTIC, CARTWHEEL BOOKS, and associated logos
are trademarks and/or registered trademarks of Scholastic Inc.

"Arts and Crafts" from *I Spy* © 1992 by Walter Wick; "Baking Cookies" and "Santa's Workshop" from *I Spy Christmas* © 1992 by Walter Wick; "Clown's Dressing Room" from *I Spy Fun House* © 1993 by Walter Wick; "The Secret Note" from *I Spy Mystery* © 1993 by Walter Wick; "Rainbow Express" and "Toy Planet" from *I Spy Fantasy* © 1994 by Walter Wick; "A Is for…" and "Sorting and Classifying" from *I Spy School Days* © 1995 by Walter Wick; "Good Morning" and "Inventor's Workshop" from *I Spy Spooky Night* © 1996 by Walter Wick; "The Treasure Chest Store" from *I Spy Treasure Hunt* © 1999 by Walter Wick. All published by Scholastic Inc.

Library of Congress card catalog number: 2002008196

ISBN 0-439-45401-8

20 19 18 17 16   07

Printed in Singapore   46
First printing, January 2003

Reinforced Binding for Library Use

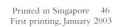

TABLE OF CONTENTS

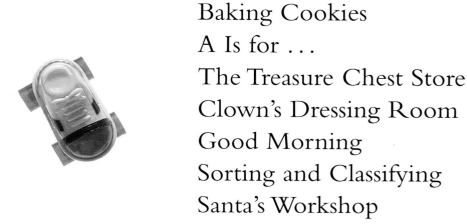

Picture riddles fill this book;
Turn the pages! Take a look!

Use your mind, use your eye;
Read the riddles — play I SPY!

I spy a clothespin, a dog, a red block,
An exclamation point, and a sock;

A yellow flag, a waterfall,
A dump-truck wheel, and a flat baseball.

I spy two boats, a bottle of glue,

A heart, a trunk, four buttons of blue;

Eight paper clips, a safety pin, SKY,
Five leaves, a crab, and a butterfly.

I spy a boot, five arrows, blue hair,
A deer, four flames, a little green bear;

Five white beards, two three-string guitars,
Six raisin eyes, and three treetop stars.

I spy a bus, six birds, a boat,
Five marbles, a match, and a musical note;

Planet Earth, three planes, an egg, a heart,
A bee, a key, a fork, and a dart.

I spy two penguins, a spinning top,

An eagle, three trains, and an old flip-flop;

A skunk, a goose, a bobby pin,
A giraffe, a deer, and a violin.

I spy a giraffe, a zebra, a boot,

A huge safety pin, a rabbit, a flute;

Scissors, bananas, a necktie with bats,
A backwards GIRL, and two spotted cats.

I spy a pencil, a hammer, two bears,

Two pigs, two lizards, and five tiny chairs;

Two bowling pins, a butterfly, and BOO,
Pliers, two deer, and a small horseshoe.

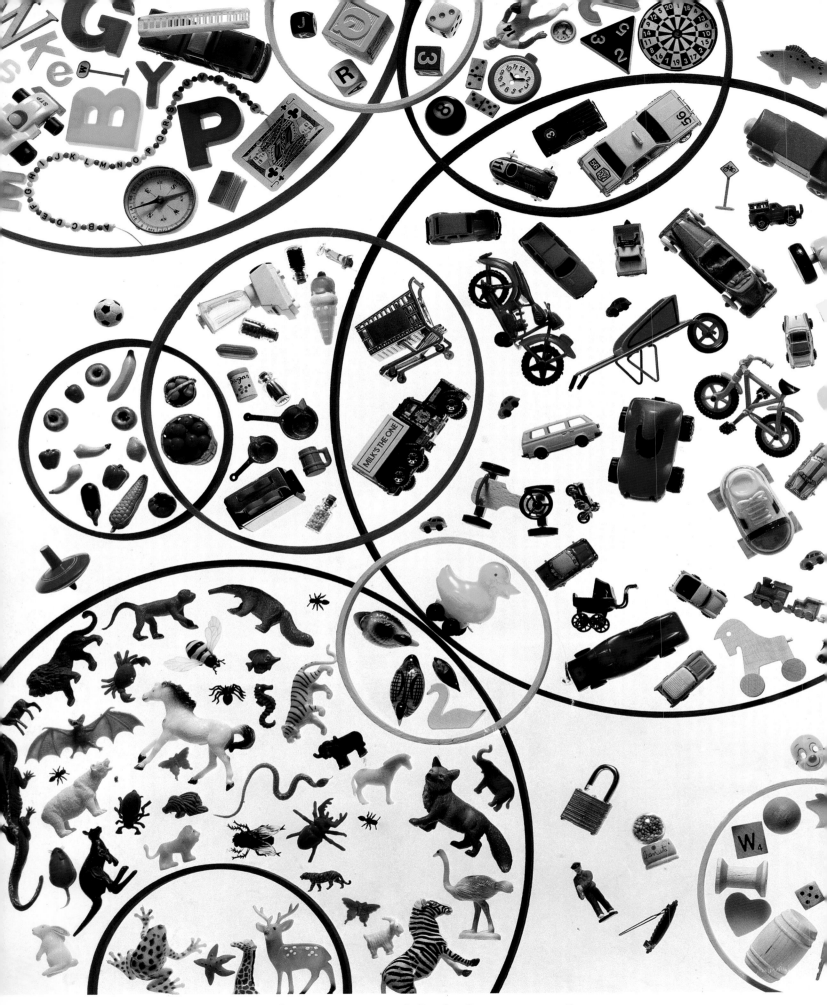

I spy a thimble, two golf clubs, a crab,

Three dogs, twin crowns, and a taxi cab;

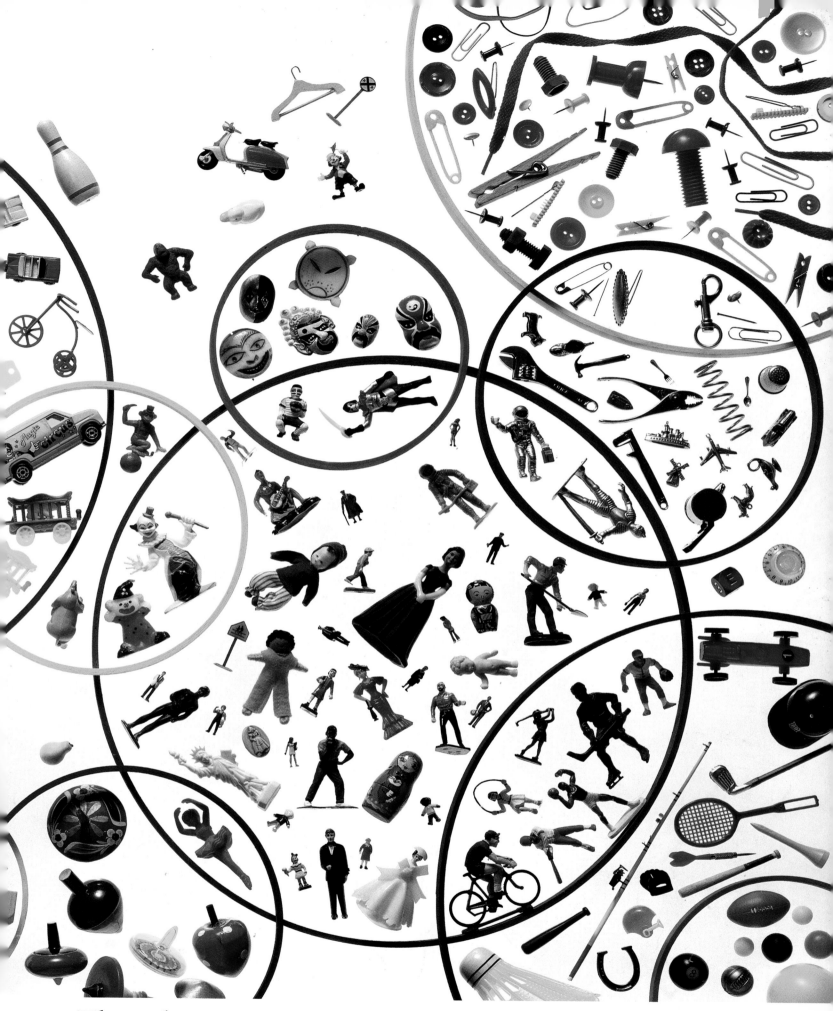

Three horses, a compass, a hanger, a goat,
Two ice-cream cones, a book, and a boat.

23

I spy two cows, two horses that rock,

A plane, a pig, a dog, and a clock;

Four wooden trees, a wooden saw handle,
A turkey, a steeple, two pipes, and a candle.

I spy a cork on a bottle, four R's,

A dinosaur, a bear, five cars;

A cherry, a football, a shovel, a pie,
A hot dog, a dart, and a dragonfly.

I spy a toothbrush, a domino,
A horseshoe, a rowboat, a radio;

A saxophone, two keys, and a bat,
A leopard, a plane, and a birthday hat.

I spy a paper clip, two shaker tops,

FROGS, two sevens, three chains, DEW DROPS;

A safety pin, glasses, a snake, two tires,
GHOST, a ghost, and a tool to cut wires.

EXTRA CREDIT RIDDLES

Find the Pictures That Go with These Riddles:

I spy two flags, a panda bear,

A hexagon, and a yellow square.

I spy three ants, CIRCUS, a bear,

A fishing pole, a pig, and a hare.

I spy a van, a ladder, a jack,

Four horses, GAMES, and a wooden track.

I spy a gear, a ladder, a bat,

A rolling pin, and a fire hat.

I spy two owls, a pretty rainbow,

A magnet, a hanger, and a small domino.

I spy a rooster, two violin bows,

A rolling pin, and a puzzle piece nose.

I spy a straw, an eraser, a dog,

Three dinosaurs, two hats, and a frog.

I spy a goat, a piece of yarn,

An old lifeboat, and an old red barn.

I spy a blue bell, a cart, a top,

A yellow cap, and a lollipop.

I spy a comb, a bracelet with moons,

A bowling pin, and four balloons.

I spy five W's, a very HOT hand,

A corkscrew, a wrench, a watch, and BRAND.

I spy a comb, a turtle shell,

A cowboy boot, and a carousel.

About the Creators of *I Spy*

Jean Marzollo has written many award-winning children's books, including twelve I Spy books and seven I Spy Little books. Her highly acclaimed science series for new readers includes *I Am Planet Earth* and *I Am a Star*, both illustrated by Judith Moffatt. She has also written: *I Love You: A Rebus Poem* and *I See a Star: A Christmas Rebus Story*, both illustrated by Suse MacDonald; *Happy Birthday, Martin Luther King*, illustrated by Brian Pinkney; *Thanksgiving Cats*, illustrated by Hans Wilhelm; *Shanna's Princess Show, Shanna's Doctor Show, Shanna's Ballerina Show*, and *Shanna's Teacher Show*, illustrated by Shane W. Evans; *Pretend You're a Cat*, illustrated by Jerry Pinkney; *Mama Mama*, illustrated by Laura Regan; *Home Sweet Home*, illustrated by Ashley Wolff; *Soccer Sam*, illustrated by Blanche Sims; and *Close Your Eyes*, illustrated by Susan Jeffers. For nineteen years, Jean Marzollo and Carol Devine Carson produced Scholastic's kindergarten magazine, *Let's Find Out*. Ms. Marzollo holds a master's degree from the Harvard Graduate School of Education. She is the 2000 recipient of the Rip Van Winkle Award presented by the School Library Media Specialists of Southeastern New York. She lives with her husband, Claudio, in New York State's Hudson Valley.

Walter Wick is the author and photographer of highly acclaimed books including *Can You See What I See?*, a *New York Times* best-seller. He also created *A Drop of Water: A Book of Science and Wonder*, which won the Boston Globe/Horn Book Award for Nonfiction, was named a Notable Children's Book by the American Library Association, and was selected as an Orbis Pictus Honor Book and a CBC/NSTA Outstanding Science Trade Book for Children. *Walter Wick's Optical Tricks*, a book of photographic illusions, was named a Best Illustrated Children's Book by *The New York Times Book Review*, was recognized as a Notable Children's Book by the American Library Association, and received many awards, including a Platinum Award from the Oppenheim Toy Portfolio, a Young Readers Award from *Scientific American*, a *Bulletin* Blue Ribbon, and a Parents' Choice Silver Honor. Mr. Wick has invented photographic games for *Games* magazine and photographed covers for books and magazines, including *Newsweek, Discover*, and *Psychology Today*. A graduate of Paier College of Art, Mr. Wick lives with his wife, Linda, in New York and Connecticut.

Carol Devine Carson, the book designer for the I Spy series, is the art director for a major publishing house in New York City.

Reviews and Praise for I Spy

For *I Spy Treasure Hunt:*

Marzollo's structured rhymes provide the clues while Wick's stunningly detailed miniature village provides the hidden answers for readers to seek out.

School Library Journal

For *I Spy Super Challenger!:*

The trademark rhyming riddles lead sharp-eyed readers to objects in crisp photographs. Wick's painstakingly prepared illustrations — bright, elaborate, and wonderfully thematic — strike a great balance between shape and color.

Booklist

For the Educational Value of the I Spy Books:

Kids find I Spy engaging because it builds on their excellent visual discrimination skills. It also challenges them incrementally with some initial success virtually guaranteed. Good teachers provide for instruction this way — and it works! Another appeal of I Spy, besides the sheer beauty of Walter Wick's photographs, is their uniqueness. They capture our attention because they are different and interesting. Brain research tells us that learners respond to novelty. As children respond to I Spy, they improve their reading, writing, rhyming, critical thinking, and vocabulary skills.

Dr. Joanne Marien, Superintendent
Somers Public Schools
Somers, New York

Acknowledgments

I'd like to thank the lively and lovely members of Girl Scout Troop 1405 for testing the I Spy riddles in this book: Michelle Cotennec, Emily Young, Elizabeth Wilcox, Meghan Spratt, Faye Rice, Katie McConville, Natalie Ely, Kelly O'Campo, and Jenn Cotennec, as well as their super smart troop leader, Donna Cotennec. Once again, I am grateful to David Marzollo for his eagle eyes, peppy persistence, and remarkable memory.

Jean Marzollo

Other I Spy books:

I SPY: A BOOK OF PICTURE RIDDLES

I SPY CHRISTMAS

I SPY FUN HOUSE

I SPY MYSTERY

I SPY FANTASY

I SPY SCHOOL DAYS

I SPY SPOOKY NIGHT

I SPY SUPER CHALLENGER!

I SPY GOLD CHALLENGER!

I SPY TREASURE HUNT

I SPY EXTREME CHALLENGER!

I SPY YEAR-ROUND CHALLENGER!

And for the youngest child:

I SPY LITTLE BOOK

I SPY LITTLE ANIMALS

I SPY LITTLE WHEELS

I SPY LITTLE CHRISTMAS

I SPY LITTLE NUMBERS

I SPY LITTLE LETTERS

I SPY LITTLE BUNNIES

I SPY LITTLE LEARNING BOX

Also available:

I SPY SCHOOL DAYS CD-ROM

I SPY SPOOKY MANSION CD-ROM

I SPY TREASURE HUNT CD-ROM

I SPY JUNIOR CD-ROM

I SPY JUNIOR: PUPPET PLAYHOUSE CD-ROM

I SPY CHALLENGER FOR GAME BOY ADVANCE